KOALAS

by Tanya Lee Stone

BLACKBIRCH®
PRESS

THOMSON

GALE

San Diego • Detroit • New York • San Francisco • Cleveland • New Haven, Conn. • Waterville, Maine • London • Munich

THOMSON

✳

GALE

© 2003 by Blackbirch Press™. Blackbirch Press™ is an imprint of The Gale Group, Inc., a division of Thomson Learning, Inc.

Blackbirch Press™ and Thomson Learning™ are trademarks used herein under license.

For more information, contact
The Gale Group, Inc.
27500 Drake Rd.
Farmington Hills, MI 48331-3535
Or you can visit our Internet site at http://www.gale.com

Photographs © 2000 by Chang Yi-Wen; page 4 © Corbis; page 5 © Corel

Cover photograph © PhotoDisc

© 2000 by Chin-Chin Publications Ltd.

No. 274-1, Sec.1 Ho-Ping E. Rd., Taipei, Taiwan, R.O.C.
Tel: 886-2-2363-3486 Fax: 886-2-2363-6081

LIBRARY OF CONGRESS CATALOGING-IN-PUBLICATION DATA

Stone, Tanya Lee.
 Koalas / by Tanya Lee Stone.
    p. cm. -- (Wild wild world)
Summary: Describes the physical characteristics, habitat, and behavior of koalas.
Includes bibliographical references.
 ISBN 1-4103-0049-8 (hardback : alk. paper)
 1. Koala--Juvenile literature. [1. Koala.] I. Title. II. Series.

QL737.M384 S77 2003
599.2'5--dc21

                                             2002152045

Printed in Taiwan
10 9 8 7 6 5 4 3 2 1

Table of Contents

About Koalas

Koalas live in Australia.

There are three kinds of koalas. Each kind comes from a specific area of Australia.

Queensland koalas are the smallest. They weigh about 15 pounds.

New South Wales koalas are medium-sized koalas.

Victoria koalas are the biggest. They can weigh up to 30 pounds.

All koalas are marsupials. A marsupial is an animal that spends the first part of its life in its mother's pouch. A female marsupial's pouch is on the outside of her body.

Queensland

New
South
Wales

Brisbane

Victoria

Sydney
Canberra

Koala Life

Koalas spend most of their time in trees. They live, eat, and sleep in the tops of eucalyptus trees.

A koala's nose is big and black. A koala has a good sense of smell and uses its nose to sniff out food and other animals.

The small tail of a koala doesn't get in its way while sitting on a tree branch.

These cute, furry animals look like bears, but they are not!

Living in Trees

Koalas have thick fur that keeps them warm and dry.

The fur on their underbelly is lighter than the rest. Males also have a scent gland on their chest. A male koala will rub his chest onto leaves and branches to mark his territory.

Koalas do not build nests in the trees. They use their strong legs and sharp claws to simply hang on to the tree branches.

Koalas stay in the trees through all kinds of weather. When its fur gets wet, a koala just shakes the water off.

Living Alone

Koalas live alone. If several koalas share a tree, they each stick to their own branch. Usually, it is only mother koalas and their babies that spend time together.

Koalas are peaceful animals. They look cuddly, but they do not like to be bothered.

Koalas only fight to defend themselves. Males may also fight during mating season.

Their sharp claws and teeth are useful when koalas need to fight. If it gets angry, a koala will let out a loud scream or cry!

Sleeping

Koalas sleep a lot—up to 18 hours a day!

To sleep, a koala holds onto a branch or snuggles into a fork in the tree so it won't fall out. Koalas can sleep in almost any position.

Sometimes they sleep with their paws curled up or folded. And sometimes they let their arms dangle out of the tree.

Eucalyptus Leaves

When a koala is not sleeping, it is eating.

Koalas mainly eat shoots and leaves from eucalyptus trees. But not all kinds of eucalyptus leaves are safe to eat. Some of the leaves are poisonous.

Koalas use their sensitive noses to tell which leaves are good to eat.

Koalas also have sharp front teeth to tear leaves from a tree. Their back teeth are flat and are perfect for grinding up the tough, chewy leaves. Koalas eat up to 2 pounds of leaves a day.

There are different kinds of eucalyptus leaves.

Koalas hardly ever drink water. They get all the moisture they need from the leaves they eat.

Excellent Climbers

Koalas are excellent tree climbers. They reach around a tree trunk with their front paws and dig their claws right into the tree. Then they pull up with their front legs and push with their back legs. They shimmy right up!

Sometimes when a koala wants to move to a different tree, it climbs down to the ground. It does this rear-end first.

Once on the ground, a koala walks on all fours. It walks slowly on the ground. But it can run quickly to the nearest tree if it is being chased.

Jumping

The other way a koala moves from tree to tree is by jumping. It just reaches over to the nearest branch, grabs hold with one paw, and leaps!

The koalas on the other page live in the zoo. They are more used to sharing a tree branch than koalas in the wild.

Strong Muscles

Koalas are very powerful animals. They have strong muscles in their shoulders, arms, and legs. This helps them climb. It also helps them hold on to a tree for long periods of time.

Their sharp, curved claws help them climb and grab on to trees.

The front paws of a koala have five claws. Three of them are located at the top of the paw while the other two are on the side.

A koala's back paws have four claws each. They can spread these claws far apart.

The dark, leathery padding on the undersides of a koala's paws helps keep it from sliding down a branch.

Baby Joeys

A baby koala is called a joey.

Most female marsupials have a pouch for their baby that opens in the front. A koala's pouch is different. It opens from the rear.

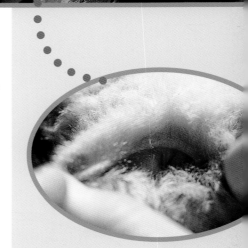

When a koala is born, it is tiny—about the size of a bean. A newborn joey is deaf, blind, and furless. It finds its way through its mother's fur and climbs into her pouch.

Safe inside, the baby nurses and grows. It does not come out until it is about 6 months old.

There are many other kinds of marsupials that live in Australia. The opposite page shows a few of them. The left column, from top to bottom, shows a bandicoot, red kangaroo, and marsupial mouse. The right column, from top to bottom, shows a wallaby, a Tasmanian devil, and a wombat.

Marsupials are the only animals in the world with this special way of caring for their young.

For More Information

Burt, Denise. *Koalas.* Minneapolis, MN: Carolrhoda Books, 1999.

Feeney, Kathy. *Koalas for Kids.* Chanhassen, MN: Northword Press, 1999.

Lee, Sandra. *Koalas.* Chanhassen, MN: Childs World, 1998.

Sotzek, Hannelore and Kalman, Bobbie. *The Koala Is Not a Bear!* New York: Crabtree, 1997.

Glossary

joey a baby koala

marsupial a group of animals whose females carry their babies in a pouch on their body